FOURTH
DOWN & LIFE

PLAYING TO WIN THE GAME

DERRICK A. WALKER

ISBN: 979-8-218-82276-7

First Edition

DEDICATION

This book is dedicated to my grandmother, Deloris Sylvia Alexander Walker, who never wavered on her love for the game of football and her beloved Washington Redskins. We have shared the special connection of football since my childhood. I cherish the moments watching the game with you, as well as your commentary. You are missed always.

ACCLAIMS

"You made me a better wide receiver...now as a coach myself, I use a lot of the drills you instilled in me."

-Adonis, High School Football Coach

"My son struggled with his releases at times, thank you for helping him get better with that part of his game."

-Brian, Parent of High School Football Player

"History was made at the Brook with you at the helm. Congrats on the first women's flag football season coach!"

-J. McKinley, High School Basketball Coach

"I'm very proud of you. You are an amazing guy! Keep it up!!"

-D. Strongarm, Local County Sheriff

"Thanks for the knowledge."

-T. Standback, Middle School Football Player

"It was most definitely a pleasure meeting you. Thank you for helping grow the game for women in football."

-J. Overstreet, Team USA Flag Football Player & MVP
3X Medalist

TABLE OF CONTENTS

INTRODUCTION

If you are taking the time to read this book, just know this book is for you. It was written for the individual who aspires to become greater. The one who is about getting results and winning in life. That person who's all about tearing the fibers and doing the work to live a fulfilling, balanced, and great life. After all, that's what we all desire right? For life to not just be good, but great!

Although Fourth Down & Life is based around the sport of football, anyone desiring to grow and produce legitimate results advancing every area of their life will benefit from tapping into this book. I did not write Fourth Down & Life as another self-help resource, but as a book to offer sustainable support and assist in thrusting you into your next chapter with confidence.

To get the most out of the information provided in this book, my recommendation is to use the "Life Drills" at the end of each chapter as daily practical tools to challenge and stretch you. Putting these drills to use will give you an advantage in any area of your life.

As far back as I can remember, I have always had football coaches impart valuable lessons I recall to this day. Thankfully, I had the pleasure of being introduced to the game of football at a young age and have been able to lean into the hard lessons football has taught me.

From the brotherhood, comradery, and companionship found through my teammates, to learning how to be coachable through the coaching staff, to doing the internal work to zero in on my skill, football has helped shape me into the person I am today. I am better because of the game. I consider myself a well-rounded, balanced human being and I believe this is partly because of the football lessons poured into me that I was able to translate off the field.

You may not have a football coach as a reference point, but we all have been gifted with someone throughout our life who has served as a guide or mentor helping us reach our next level.

Maybe your "coach" was a teacher, a community leader, an older sibling or cousin, a pastor, or a supervisor. Outside of football coaches, I have had my parents, grandparents, extended family, teachers, spiritual leaders, and homies keep me inspired and focused. They have been a part of my "team" offering support and guidance when faced with life's hardships.

I've always believed football is a microcosm of life. Spend

time with any football player and they will share special memories of the game that taught them life lessons they refer to until this day. Whether you've played football or not, it's my pleasure to take the life lessons I've gleaned from football over the last 30 plus years, whether I was playing or coaching, and share them with you.

My hope is that you will take hold of the tips, instructions, and advice offered in this book and personalize it to your own life's journey. Take seriously the Life Drills provided. Put them to use.

Do the work and I promise that you, and everyone connected to you, will be better because of it. Expect from this day forward to step into the world everyday with increased confidence and clarity.

We are on life's journey together. Let's continue to crush our goals, move in life with precision, accumulate wins, and become an even greater human being. Tap in!

CHAPTER 1

COMMUNICATION

Communication is an essential part of the game of football. Communication happens in several ways. It is not just one person speaking to another and it ends there. Communication is also understanding and processing what has been communicated to you. Let's look at this essential topic further in the context of the game of football.

Before the ball is snapped, a quarterback will have to communicate to his offensive teammates. The quarterback receives the play call communication from the coach on the sideline. Once received, the quarterback's job is to now communicate the play call to his offensive teammates in the huddle before they get set on the line of scrimmage to run the play. The quarterback must be able to clearly and concisely translate the communication from the coach to his offensive teammates. Now, for this communication to be effective, his offensive teammates must be able to receive the communication from him and process it successfully. If the quarterback does not accurately and precisely communicate the play to his offensive teammates, things can go horribly wrong once the ball is snapped and the play begins. A breakdown in communication can cost a team an entire game all because communication was simply not well executed. This meticulous level of communication doesn't just apply to the quarterback, but goes across the board from the coaches on the sideline to the players on the field, including offense and defense. The purpose is to not just communicate, but to execute effective communication. This is what leads to success and to winning games, which is the ultimate goal.

Translating the skill of communication over to life is simple. For one to experience profound success in various aspects of their life, this same high-level of communication must be executed daily. Effective communication is needed whether interacting with a teacher, a business partner, a classmate, a friend, or anyone you may come in contact with throughout your day. Communication needs to be concise, clear, and understandable so the person on the receiving end can process what is being expressed and make best use of it. This will put you in the best position to win in most situations. Effective communication truly matters.

Life Drills: Strengthening Communication

1) Daily Check-In Drill

Spend 5–10 minutes each day asking someone close to you how they're really doing. Listen actively with no interruptions and no advice at first. Focus on understanding what they are expressing without focusing on responding.

2) **Mirror Practice Drill**

Before delivering an important message, practice saying it out loud to yourself or in front of a mirror. This helps clarify your words, tone, and body language.

3) **Active Listening Drill**

During a conversation, consciously repeat back what the other person said in your own words before responding. Example: "So what I hear you saying is..." This ensures clarity and shows respect.

4) **One-Hit Feedback Drill**

Each day, give one piece of constructive feedback or positive reinforcement to someone. Keep the feedback or reinforcement clear and specific. Try to focus on behavior and not their personality.

5) **The Pause Drill**

Before responding to a conflict or emotionally charged message, pause for three breaths. This prevents reactive communication and gives space for thoughtful responses.

CHAPTER 2

HANDLING ADVERSITY

There is no escaping adversity in the game of football. Adversity sets in from the moment you begin preparing for a game. Adversity starts at practice. Football practices can be grueling, repetitive, and even boring at times. Despite these challenges, one must stay locked in and focused on the task of preparing for the game. Adversity easily creeps in when one's mind is no longer focused on preparation tasks and one no longer desires to do the work but is in a hurry to get to the fun part, which is playing the game. The question is, how does one handle the hard times, the times when things are not perfect, when things are not what they want them to be and what was once a passion is no longer exciting? How is adversity handled? Let's dive into a football game situation and see how one can handle adversity.

Let's say Team A has spent all week preparing for an opponent. Team A has a great game plan. They have watched film and studied their opponent. They are confident in their game plan, as well as confident in themselves. Team A knows that if they can execute their game plan, they can win the game against Team B.

It's now game day. Team A comes out ready to play, but on the first play of the game Team A throws an interception to

Team B and Team B runs it back for a touchdown. Now Team A is down 7-0 early in the game. Team A then comes out with their second possession and fumbles the ball. Team B recovers the ball and a few plays later Team B scores again. Now the score is 14-0 with Team A losing the game. At this point, it's almost guaranteed that Team A did not have in their game plan they would be down 14-0 early in the game.

Now Team A is facing major adversity. The question instantly becomes, how does Team A handle this adversity? Do they waste energy whining and complaining about their circumstances? Do they cry about it? Do they pray about it? Do they come together as a group and start to figure out a new plan to overcome this newfound adversity? There are many ways Team A could choose to handle this adversity; however, what it really comes down to are two main options: 1)They can respond positively, working as a team to overcome and still find a way to win the game; or 2) they can respond negatively and let the adversity overtake them causing them to lose the game.

Life can be very much the same way in how adversity can ambush you and catch you off guard. You can have a solid game plan, and unexpectedly life will intercept your first pass, up the score, put you down, and throw you off your game plan.

Life indeed can have you feeling like "woe is me". However, it's not what life will throw at you or the adversity you face that matters the most. It is how you respond to that adversity. Do you respond with positive emotions or with negative emotions? How you respond will ultimately determine your outcome concerning adverse situations.

Life Drills: Handling Adversity

1. **Adversity Journal Drill**

    Each time you face a setback, write down what happened, how it made you feel, and one lesson you can take from it. Review weekly to track growth in resilience.

2. **Controlled Stress Exposure Drill**

    Put yourself in a small, safe challenge you'd normally avoid—like cold showers, timed exercises, or public speaking practice. Gradually building tolerance to discomfort strengthens your response to bigger setbacks.

3. **The "Next Play" Drill**

    After any failure or mistake, immediately write down the next step you can take to move forward. Treat every challenge like a football play: don't dwell on the hit—plan your next move.

4.   **Perspective Reset Drill**

When adversity hits, list three positive things that are still going well in your life. This builds mental resilience and prevents you from spiraling.

5.   **Support Huddle Drill**

Identify a trusted mentor, friend, or teammate and share a current challenge. Ask for one piece of advice or encouragement. Adversity is easier to handle when you don't face it alone.

CHAPTER 3

SITUATIONAL FOOTBALL

D ring a 60-minute football game, the landscape is ever changing. The situations in which a team must execute are always unknown until after the end of each play. For instance, a team will start with a 1st down; however once that 1st down play has been completed only then can that team determine what the next move will be. Ideally, offense would like things to stay on schedule. This means the ball is consistently moving forward at a good pace of yards, gaining approximately 4-6 yards per play. Even with that hope, things can get behind schedule, such as plays ending with negative yards which puts a team in down and long situations. A good coach must always pay attention to the situation his team is in, even if it's not an ideal position.

Here are some main factors to be considered in a live football game regarding situational football and how decisions are made:

- What down is it and how many yards are needed to gain the next 1st down?

- What quarter is it?

- How much time is remaining on the clock?

- Which yard line is the ball on?

- Is the team in plus territory (the opponent's side of the field), or is the team in negative territory (their own side of the field)?

These major factors must be considered when a coach is deciding what to do in any given situation during the course of a football game. Interestingly enough, considering those major factors, plus a few others, making a decision must be done in a fairly quick time frame. How a coach is able to handle themselves and make a good decision can determine the outcome of a game. The situations in a football game are constantly changing; therefore, a team and coach must be focused on, not just plays, but situations in which to use plays.

Situations in life can change very quickly as well. Adapting to those situations and being flexible is a great trait to have in life. When things are too rigid, they can break. If things are too loose, they also can break if they are inherently brittle. Having the ability to operate in both balance and flexibility in life helps anyone to adapt and adjust to the various situations life will throw at you.

You should often assess your life's situations. Take some time to consider whatever major factors you may have going on so you can make a quick, wise, and winning decision for your life.

Life Drills: Situational Football

1.   Down & Distance Drill

At the start of each day, identify your "down and distance." Is today about gaining small yards (steady work) or going deep (big risks)? Adjust your mindset and strategy to match.

2.   Two-Minute Drill

Give yourself two minutes to make a decision on something small you've been delaying. This trains you to act confidently under pressure.

3.   Red Zone Drill

Choose one task that's close to completion and finish it today. If you're unable to complete the task today, give yourself a realistic deadline, then create a realistic plan to

complete the task. Like the red zone, it's about closing the deal, not starting over.

4.   Punt or Go For It Drill

When faced with a choice, ask: *Is this the time to take the risk, or should I wait?* Write down your reasoning. Over time, you'll sharpen your decision-making.

5. **Clock Awareness Drill**

    Set specific time limits for tasks or conversations. This builds urgency and helps you avoid dragging things out when the situation requires speed.

CHAPTER 4

TAKING THE HITS

In football, every player knows the hits are coming. No matter how strong your stance, how sharp your eyes, or how well prepared your game plan, the impact is inevitable.

Whether a linebacker crashes into you mid-route, a defensive end blindsides you, or you collide helmet-to-helmet with someone just as determined to make a play, you will feel the hit. Some hits knock you off balance. Others drop you flat on your back. But the true test isn't whether you get hit, it's how you respond when you do.

Life works the same way. As you continue to live, experiencing hits and their impacts are inevitable. Hits come in different forms, such as losing a job you thought was secure, failing a class you studied hard for, a relationship breaking down, death of a loved-one, or a dream slipping just out of reach. Like football, you rarely see all of them coming, but you know they are part of the "game of life". Some arrive softly, like a bump that nudges you off track, while others shake your world leaving you gasping for breath. And just like on the field, you don't get to choose whether you take hits, you only get to choose how you handle them.

Hitting is simply part of the game. Coaches don't tell players to avoid contact. Instead, they train them to withstand it, absorb it, and even use it to their advantage. The same goes for life. Struggles, setbacks, and disappointments aren't detours, they are built into the journey. Pretending they won't come only makes the fall harder and more painful when they arrive. Expecting them, preparing for them, and adjusting to them builds resilience.

Every football player who has been knocked down has heard the same sideline wisdom: *"Get up and line up again."* The game doesn't pause to give you time to sulk. Life doesn't either. When you get knocked down in life, the clock keeps running. The bills don't stop coming, opportunities don't wait, and responsibilities don't fade. Rising after a hit takes courage, but staying down ensures defeat.

The hits during football games teach an important lesson each time:

1. How to better protect yourself

2. How to more clearly read defenses

3. How to anticipate what's coming next

Hits in life teach the same lessons. A failed project teaches you about preparation. A broken relationship teaches you about communication and self-awareness. A missed opportunity sharpens your hunger for the next one. A valuable lesson to hold on to is that pain is often a better teacher than comfort. Although the average person doesn't willingly accept pain, it indeed challenges your ability to survive and makes you stronger when you get on the other side of the situation that caused the pain. Comfort keeps you stagnant and doesn't allow you to tap into your real strength.

In the game of football, you're not just a receiver of hits, you're also expected to deliver them. Not out of malice, but as part of the game. In life, the expectation of delivering hits consists of holding people accountable, standing firm on your values, or pushing yourself beyond limits when everything inside you says quit. Sometimes the strongest "hits" you deliver are to your own fears, doubts, and excuses.

No champion ever made it through a football season untouched. Every scar, bruise, and sore muscle is a reminder that they were in the fight. Life's no different. The people who achieve their goals aren't the ones who avoid pain. They are the ones who endure it, grow through it, and keep moving forward.

So, the question isn't *if* you will take hits in football or in life, it's *when*. And when they come, you get to decide whether you will stay on the ground or if you will rise, line back up, and keep playing the game.

In the end, greatness isn't defined by how many times you avoid being hit. It's defined by how many times you take the hit, rise again, and keep pushing toward the end zone of your life.

Life Drills: Practicing Resilience Off The Field

1. Bounce-Back Journaling Drill

Write down one "hit" you've taken recently (big or small). Then write how you got back up—or how you plan to. Track your bounce-back moments weekly to see your resilience grow.

2. Controlled Contact Drill

Football players practice taking hits in drills so they're ready for game day. In life, simulate smaller challenge intentionally: take a cold shower, fast from social media, or push through one extra workout set. Training in discomfort builds resilience for bigger hits.

3. **Post-Hit Reflection Drill**

After a setback, pause and ask: *What did this hit teach me? How can I adjust my game plan?* Turning pain into feedback ensures you grow stronger, not bitter.

4. **The Get-Up Rule Drill**

Make a personal rule: whenever you face a hit—criticism, rejection, failure—allow yourself no more than 24 hours to process it. After that, stand up, reset, and move forward.

5. **Hit & Response Drill**

For one week, every time something frustrates you (traffic, mistakes, conflict), consciously choose your response instead of reacting emotionally. Track how often you stayed in control.

CHAPTER 5

THE GAME IS TIMED

In football, the difference between a championship play and a devastating mistake can come down to a fraction of a second. Timing isn't just a technicality, it's everything. One of the clearest examples of this is the snap count.

When a quarterback lines up behind the center, he initiates the play with a cadence, a rhythm of calls and counts designed to signal his teammates when to move. Every player must be in sync, waiting for the exact right moment to spring into action. Jump early, and it's a penalty. React too late, and you might miss your block, your route, or your opportunity.

This rhythm, this waiting for the right moment to move, mirrors a fundamental truth about life: Success often depends not just on what you do, but *when* you do it. How many times in life do we act too soon? We leap into relationships because we're tired of waiting. We accept the first job offer because we're afraid nothing better will come. We speak out of emotion rather than reason, only to regret what was said in swiftness.

On the other hand, there are times we wait too long. We hesitate to say how we feel. We delay chasing our dreams until "the time is right," not realizing that perfect conditions rarely exist. In both football and life, mistimed action can cost us dearly.

Football trains players to live in the tension between readiness and restraint. You must be alert and prepared to move, but also grounded in the discipline of waiting. The lineman doesn't just react to the sound of the quarterback's voice, he listens for the right cue. In life, we must learn to listen the same way for the signs, the timing, the alignment of our preparation with the opportunity.

Consider the 2-minute drill during the game when a team has little time and must act quickly but efficiently. There's no room for panic. Decisions must be made fast, but not carelessly. This scenario represents life in crunch time. When it's time for a job interview after weeks of preparation, or it's time to have a tough conversation you've avoided, there's a life-changing choice you have to make under pressure. The best outcomes come from those who have trained for the moment and trust their instincts without rushing.

Ultimately, football teaches us that timing is not just a matter of chance, it's a skill built from repetition, awareness, and discipline. Whether you're waiting for the right moment to start a project, tell someone you love them, or make a big move, remember this: the great ones don't just play hard. They play *on time.*

Life Drills: The Game Is Timed

1. **Two-Minute Drill**

   Each morning, write down your top three priorities for the day. Like a two-minute offense, stay focused on scoring points that matter instead of wasting plays.

2. **Film the Clock Drill**

   Track how you spend your time for one full day. At the end, review your day like film study. Where are you wasting time? Where can you be more efficient?

3. **Timeout Strategy Drill**

   Football teams use timeouts strategically. Schedule short breaks during your day to reset your mind instead of burning out.

4. **Fourth Quarter Focus Drill**

   At night, ask yourself: *If today were my last quarter, did I use it well?* This reflection builds urgency and gratitude for the time you still have.

5.   Play Clock Drill

Set a timer for 25 minutes and work on a single task with no distractions. Like managing the play clock, this trains you to maximize each possession of your time.

CHAPTER 6

YOU HAVE TO STAY FOCUSED

In football, the play can change in an instant. A quarterback has seconds to read a defense, a receiver must time his cut with the precision of a dancer, and a linebacker has to react without hesitation. What separates good players from great ones isn't always talent, it is mental focus.

Imagine being in a stadium with 70,000 fans screaming, coaches yelling in your ear, reading hand signals, and your own pulse pounding like a drum. Now, imagine trying to remember your assignment, read a defense, and execute your job, all in a matter of seconds. This is the environment in which football players must maintain mental clarity. It's chaos, controlled only by the discipline of focus.

In life, the chaos is different but just as real. It's the constant buzz of text messages, deadlines, conversations, and worries. When life throws a blitz your way it's easy to lose focus on what really matters, your goals, your values, your purpose. Like a quarterback under pressure, it's essential that you learn to tune out the noise and lock in on what's important.

Athletes train their bodies relentlessly, but the best athletes also train their mind. Quarterbacks spend hours in film rooms not just to understand the game, but to anticipate it. They visualize

31

scenarios, rehearse reactions, and build mental resilience.

In everyday life, mental focus can be trained the same way. Whether you're preparing for an exam, in the process of starting a major project, or simply trying to be more present in your relationships, the ability to lock in mentally is critical. Meditation, journaling, time-blocking, or setting daily intentions are all forms of mental conditioning. Just like strength grows with repetition and discipline, so does focus.

Football teaches you that every second counts. One lapse in focus, leading to a missed tackle or a dropped ball, can cost a team the game. The same goes for life. A text message, DM, or phone call might cause you to miss a valuable in-person moment with someone you care about. Letting your mind wander during class or an information session could mean missing the one idea that changes everything.

Football also teaches that mistakes are not the end, they're just the next down. Mental focus isn't about being perfect. It's about recovering quickly. Did you just get beat on a play? Lock back in and win the next play. The same rule applies in life. You may slip up, lose your way, or let distractions take over, but what matters is how quickly you refocus.

In the fourth quarter, when legs are tired and minds are foggy, the difference between winners and losers comes down to mental toughness. Players with true focus dig deep, recall their training, and execute when it matters most.

Life has fourth quarters also, such as those high-stakes moments when you're tested. For example, job interviews, critical conversations, and fork in the road tough decisions are moments when your mental focus can tip the scales.

Football doesn't just teach you to focus, it demands focus. The same principles that help a player read a blitz or make a game-winning catch can help you stay sharp in your own life. Stay present. Train your mind. Trust your preparation. Learn from mistakes. And above all, when the pressure hits, remember to keep your eyes on the ball.

Life Drills: Sharpening Focus

1. Single-Task Drill

Pick one task and commit to working on it for 25 minutes without distractions (phone on silent, notifications off). Gradually increase focus time using this Pomodoro-style approach.

2. Distraction Log Drill

For one day, write down every distraction that interrupts your focus. At the end of the day, identify patterns and plan how to reduce or eliminate them.

3. Mindfulness Pause Drill

Spend 3–5 minutes each morning practicing deep breathing or meditation. This trains your brain to stay present and resist wandering thoughts.

4. Priority Drill

Each morning, list your top three tasks for the day. Focus exclusively on completing them before moving to less important items.

5. Environment Optimization Drill

Adjust your workspace or surroundings to reduce distractions—organize your desk, control noise, and remove unnecessary visual clutter.

CHAPTER 7

ARE YOU DISCIPLINED?

Ask any football coach what separates good players from great ones, and you'll almost always hear the same word: **discipline**. Talent might get you noticed, speed might win you a few plays, and strength might carry you through a season, but discipline is what sustains success. Without it, even the most gifted athlete eventually fades.

Life isn't any different. Dreams, talent, and ambition are powerful, but without discipline, they rarely reach their full potential. Discipline is the quiet engine behind every victory, on the field and off.

On the football field, discipline shows up in ways that outsiders rarely notice. It's the wide receiver running a crisp route even when he knows the ball isn't coming his way because he understands that his movement pulls defenders and opens space for someone else. It's the offensive lineman staying perfectly still until the snap count, resisting the urge to jump early even though he's charged with adrenaline. It's the safety who spends hours studying film, so he knows the quarterback's tendencies before the play even unfolds. Discipline is the player who wakes up at 5 a.m. to lift weights, runs sprints after practice, and watches his diet when everyone else is grabbing fast food. It's not glamorous, and most of the self-control work happens away from the spotlight. But when the game is on the line, discipline is what keeps a team from collapsing.

In life, discipline looks much the same, though the "plays" are different. Discipline is the student setting aside time to study when friends are out having fun. It's the parents working long hours to provide stability for their family, resisting the temptation to quit when things get hard. It's the entrepreneur saving and reinvesting rather than spending recklessly.

Discipline is following through on commitments long after the feeling of excitement has worn off. It's waking up early when you would rather sleep in, choosing healthy habits over quick fixes, and staying focused on long-term goals instead of chasing shortcuts.

One of the greatest lessons football teaches is that you cannot rely on emotion alone. A player fired up by a pregame speech might come out swinging, but if his energy isn't channeled by discipline, it fades fast. Emotions are temporary. Discipline is consistent.

In life, the same principle holds true. Motivation may get you started, but discipline keeps you moving when motivation disappears. Successful people aren't always the most inspired, they're the ones who do what needs to be done, even when they don't feel like it.

In both football and life, discipline shows up in the small, daily choices. A missed workout here, a sloppy rep there, or a skipped responsibility might not seem like much in the moment, but small cracks widen over time. By the same token, small disciplined choices build momentum. One extra rep in the weight room. One more page in the textbook. One more hour invested in your dream. Success isn't built in a day; it's built daily.

Discipline doesn't just keep you on track, it gives you freedom. The disciplined quarterback can trust his mechanics under pressure because he's drilled them thousands of times. The disciplined student enjoys more opportunities because they've built the habit of excellence. The disciplined worker has the freedom to build a career instead of just holding a job. Discipline is the bridge between potential and performance, between who you are and who you could be.

In football, discipline is the difference between a winning season and a wasted one. In life, it's the difference between living with regret and living with purpose. Every day presents a choice, to either give in to comfort or commit to discipline.

No one drifts into greatness by accident. Just like a football team must practice relentlessly, watch film diligently, and execute plays with precision, we must live intentionally if we want to see growth.

So, whether you're stepping onto the field or walking into the challenges of everyday life, remember...talent might open the door, but only discipline will keep you in the game.

Life Drills: Practicing Discipline Off the Field

1. Early Start Drill

Set your alarm 30 minutes earlier than usual for the next week. Use that time for something productive—exercise, journaling, prayer, or reading. Winning starts before the day begins.

2. Film Study for Life Drill

Just like athletes watch game film, spend 15 minutes each night reviewing your day. What did you do well? Where did you slip up? What can you improve tomorrow?

3. No-Excuse Rep Drill

Pick one area of your life—fitness, study, or work—and commit to one "extra rep" daily. One more push-up, one more page read, one more call made. Small reps build lasting habits.

4. Discipline Under Pressure Drill

Identify one habit you usually let slide when you're tired or stressed (e.g., eating healthy, sticking to your budget, finishing chores). For the next 7 days, refuse to let pressure dictate your actions.

5. The Accountability Huddle Drill

Find a teammate in life—a friend, mentor, or colleague—who will be willing to check in with you weekly. Share your goals, report your progress, and invite them to hold you accountable.

CHAPTER 8

THE HUDDLE MATTERS

In football, the huddle is more than just a circle of players clustered together on the field. It's where clarity, unity, and direction are formed in the middle of chaos. A quarterback calls the play, teammates confirm assignments, and every player leaves that huddle knowing their role. Without a huddle, confusion takes over, mistakes multiply, and the game falls apart.

Life has its own version of the huddle, which are the people you surround yourself with. Your circle—the friends, mentors, teammates, colleagues, and family you keep close—has the power to either lift you up or pull you down. Just like a team can't win with a broken huddle, you can't thrive if your circle doesn't align with your purpose.

Great football teams are built on trust. Every player in the huddle must believe that their teammate will run the right route, block the right defender, or execute the right read. Without that trust, plays collapse.

Your huddle is your inner circle of trust in life. The people you allow close to you influence your mindset, your choices, and even your future. A strong huddle pushes you toward discipline, accountability, and growth. A weak one pulls you toward excuses, negativity, and wasted potential.

Not everyone deserves a spot in your huddle. Some people drain your energy, sow division, or celebrate when you fall. Others sharpen you, speak truth even when it's uncomfortable, and push you to reach higher. Learning who belongs in your huddle, and who doesn't, is one of the most important life decisions you'll ever make.

When it comes to huddles, a key component to point out is that a huddle only works if communication is clear. In football, one misunderstood call can lead to disaster. In life, miscommunication breaks trust and damages relationships. The best huddles are built on honest words, careful listening, and a shared commitment to understanding one another.

Some players think they can do it all themselves, skipping the huddle and running their own plays. But football is a team sport, and life is much the same. Success may look individual from the outside, but it's always built on the strength of a team, such as coaches, friends, mentors, and supporters who played a role along the way.

The huddle reminds us that no matter how gifted we are, we can't win alone. The right huddle amplifies your strengths, covers your weaknesses, and helps you face the hits of life with courage. When your huddle is strong, you walk into challenges with confidence—because you know you're not walking alone.

Life Drills: Practicing Teamwork and Building Your Huddle

1. Circle Audit Drill

Write down the five people you spend the most time with. Ask: *Do they push me to grow or hold me back? Do they drain me or energize me?* Decide who belongs in your huddle and who might need to move to the sidelines.

2. Build Your Huddle Drill

Identify one person you admire or want to learn from. Reach out, ask questions, or spend more intentional time with them. Strengthen your circle by adding people who make you better.

3. Weekly Huddle Check-In Drill

Once a week, connect with your closest circle—whether in

person, by call, or message. Share wins, challenges, and goals. Keep communication open like a team reviewing film together.

4. Encouragement Rep Drill

Each day, give one teammate (friend, family member, or colleague) a word of encouragement. Small boosts build trust and unity in your huddle.

5. No Lone Wolf Drill

Pick one current challenge you've been trying to handle alone. Share it with someone in your huddle and invite their support. Practicing teamwork in small struggles builds confidence for bigger ones.

CHAPTER 9

THE PLAYBOOK

No football team takes the field without a playbook. The playbook gives structure, provides options, and keeps everyone aligned toward a common goal. It's the collection of strategies, formations, and assignments that turn chaos into order. Without it, eleven players would move in different directions, and the game would unravel instantly.

Life also requires a playbook. Without a plan, we drift. Without goals, we waste energy. Without preparation, we panic when adversity hits. Just like a football team needs a playbook to know what to run next, we need a playbook in life to guide our daily choices and long-term direction.

A football playbook prepares players for countless scenarios: third-and-long, red-zone offense, two-minute drills. Coaches don't wait until game day to figure things out; they anticipate challenges in advance.

In life, we can do the same. A personal "life playbook" helps us face tough decisions with clarity. It helps us avoid being reactive, and tossed around by emotions or circumstances. With a playbook, we approach challenges with confidence because we already know our response.

When a team practices its plays repeatedly, execution becomes automatic. The quarterback doesn't freeze when the defense blitzes. He simply falls back on what's in the playbook.

In life, preparation saves us from panic. The student who studies consistently is less likely to crumble before an exam. The worker who sharpens their skills does not fear layoffs because their skill is transferable, so they will be able to make an income elsewhere. The person who plans their finances does not break under surprise expenses. Preparation does not eliminate challenges, but it does change how we face them.

The best playbooks aren't rigid, they adapt. A quarterback may call an audible at the line of scrimmage, adjusting to what the defense shows. In life, we need the same flexibility. Plans may change, dreams may shift, and sometimes we have to adjust on the fly. A strong playbook allows freedom to adapt without abandoning the bigger vision.

A playbook is useless if it stays on the shelf. Players must study it, memorize it, and execute it under pressure. Furthermore, in life it's not enough to write down goals or make plans. Execution is key. It separates dreamers from doers.

Your playbook isn't about perfection. It's about direction.

It's a tool to help you stay focused, anticipate obstacles, and keep moving forward with purpose. Without it, life feels like sand slipping through your fingers. With it, every step carries intention.

Life Drills: Building and Executing Your Playbook

1. Write Your Game Plan Drill

Take 15 minutes and write down your top three priorities for the next month. Be specific (e.g., "Save $300," "Work out 4 days a week," "Read one book"). This becomes your short-term playbook.

2. Three-Play Priorities Drill

Each morning, write your top three goals for the day—the "plays" you must run to win today. Don't end the day until they're completed.

3. Weekly Film Review Drill

At the end of the week, review what went well and what didn't. Adjust your game plan for the next week, just like coaches refine the playbook after each game.

4. Audible Drill

Practice flexibility: when something doesn't go as planned during the week, pause and ask, *What's my best audible here?* Instead of quitting the play, adjust it.

5. Accountability Partner Drill

Share your playbook (monthly or weekly goals) with a trusted teammate—friend, mentor, or coach. Let them check in with you, just like players hold each other accountable in film study.

CHAPTER 10

ATTENTION TO DETAILS

In football, games are often won or lost on the smallest details. A quarterback reads the defense and notices a subtle shift in a linebacker's stance. A receiver catches a ball by adjusting his fingers by mere inches. An offensive lineman maintains perfect hand placement to hold the line. These tiny details—almost invisible to the untrained eye—makes the difference between victory and defeat.

Life operates quite the same. Success rarely comes from grand gestures alone. It's built on consistent attention to the small, often overlooked details. Paying attention to details can prevent mistakes, uncover opportunities, and set you apart from others who only see the surface.

Missing a detail in football, like failing to notice a defender creeping toward the end zone, can lead to a costly turnover. In life, missing details can cost you things you value, such as relationships, money, and credibility. Double checking your work, listening carefully, and noticing subtle cues are all examples of attention to detail in action.

Attention to detail isn't a natural talent, it's a habit that must be formed. Coaches train players to slow down, observe, and internalize patterns. They watch film repeatedly, practice techniques, and rehearse drill fundamentals until the smallest adjustments become second nature. Similarly, cultivating awareness in life requires deliberate focus, repetition, and reflection.

It's easy to assume the small stuff doesn't matter. But in football and life alike, neglecting details accumulates into bigger problems. The player who ignores fundamentals ends up on the bench, just as the person who overlooks small errors ends up with lost opportunities. Excellence demands intentional care in the little things.

Mastering details compounds over time. A quarterback who notices defensive tendencies early gains a strategic edge. An employee who double-checks work builds a reputation for reliability. A student who consistently and carefully reads instructions avoid preventable mistakes. Small habits create big results.

Attention to detail isn't about perfectionism, but about awareness, responsibility, and preparation. It's the difference between going through life passively and engaging fully. Just as a game is made up of thousands of tiny plays, life is made up of countless small choices—and each choice matters.

Life Drills: Sharpening Attention to Details

1. Film Room Drill

Watch a video, TV show, or news clip and write down five small details others might miss. Practice noticing what most people overlook.

2. Checklist Drill

For any task—work, school, or daily routines—create a simple checklist and follow it precisely. Train yourself to avoid skipping even small steps.

3. Observation Walk Drill

Take a 10-minute walk and note 10 details you normally wouldn't notice: colors, sounds, patterns, or behaviors. Sharpen your environmental awareness.

4. Double-Check Drill

After completing a task, review it at least twice before considering it done. Build the habit of catching errors before they cause problems.

5. Listening Drill

In conversations, focus on small verbal cues, tone, and body language. Try summarizing what was said afterward, including subtle details you might have missed.

CHAPTER 11

WHO CAN MAKE A BIG PLAY!

In football, a "big play" is a moment that can change the momentum of a game. For instance, a 50-yard touchdown pass, a perfectly timed sack, or a game-saving interception can cause a major shift in the game. Big plays don't happen by accident. They are the result of preparation, awareness, discipline, timing, teamwork, and courage. Every player on the field contributes, but the athletes who make the biggest plays seize the moment and fully commit.

Life is no different. Big opportunities, such as landing a dream job, pitching a transformative idea, repairing a strained relationship, or taking a risk that changes your path, requires preparation, courage, and focus. These moments are rare, but they define careers, relationships, and personal growth.

In football, big plays often look spontaneous, but they are the product of hours of practice and study. The quarterback doesn't just throw deep by luck. The team has practiced that route, read the defense, and timed the play hundreds of times.

In life, opportunity favors the prepared. Success rarely comes from waiting for luck. It comes from putting in the work so that when the right moment arises, you're ready to act. Big plays require courage. Even the best-prepared player must overcome fear of failure, injury, or judgment to commit fully. Hesitation can turn a potential game-winning touchdown into a missed opportunity.

In life, courage operates the same. Risking failure, speaking up, or stepping outside your comfort zone can be intimidating, but without courage big opportunities remain out of reach.

No single player makes a big play entirely alone. Timing, coordination, and trust in teammates are essential. A running back doesn't score without the offensive line opening a lane, just as a quarterback doesn't complete a long pass without a receiver running the right route.

In life, big accomplishments are rarely solo efforts. Surround yourself with people who support, guide, and challenge you. Keep in mind that timing, coordination, and shared effort turn preparation into results.

It's important to note that not every attempt results in a big play. In football, sometimes the quarterback throws an incomplete pass, just as in life a risky decision doesn't pan out. What matters is learning from mistakes and staying ready for the next opportunity. Resilience ensures that one failed attempt doesn't stop you from making the next game-changing play.

Big plays aren't just about the moment, they're about everything leading up to it: preparation, discipline, awareness, timing, courage, and teamwork. By focusing on fundamentals and staying ready, you increase your chances of turning critical opportunities into defining successes.

Life Drills: Making Big Plays

1. **Preparation Drill**

   Identify one area of life where you want a "big play" (career, fitness, relationship, personal growth). Create a detailed plan and practice consistently. Preparation builds confidence.

2. **Risk-Taking Drill**

   Each week, take one small calculated risk outside your comfort zone. Reflect afterward: what did you learn, and how can you apply it next time?

3. **Timing Practice Drill**

   Review your weekly schedule and identify the best times to tackle high-impact tasks. Acting at the right moment multiplies results.

4. Courage Visualization Drill

Spend 5 minutes imagining a high-pressure situation and visualize yourself acting confidently and decisively. This trains your mind to perform under pressure.

5. Teamwork Drill

Identify one goal where collaboration could create a "big play." Reach out to a teammate, colleague, or mentor, and plan how you'll execute together. This helps keep teamwork at the front of your mind as you work towards making big plays.

CHAPTER 12

BE COACHABLE

In football, talent gets you noticed, but being coachable keeps you on the field. Every great player, whether a rookie learning the basics or a veteran sharpening skills, must be willing to listen, adjust, and grow. Coaches look for athletes who embrace feedback, apply corrections, and respond with effort rather than ego. The ability to be coachable turns potential into progress.

Life follows the same rule. No matter how skilled, experienced, or confident we become, there is always more to learn. Being coachable means staying humble enough to receive feedback, wise enough to reflect on it, and disciplined enough to put it into practice.

In football, players who think they already "know it all" often hit a ceiling. The best athletes are humble and understand they can always get better. In life, humility works the same way. When we approach situations with openness instead of arrogance, we invite growth and opportunity.

Being coachable requires listening fully before responding. A player who interrupts the coach misses vital instructions. In life, whether at school, at work, in a relationship, or desiring personal growth, listening carefully to advice or feedback ensures we understand before reacting.

When it comes to being coachable, hearing the advice is only step one. Applying the advice is what makes the difference. A coach can give pointers all day, but if the player doesn't make the adjustment the lesson is wasted. In life, putting feedback into action, even through small adjustments, shows maturity and commitment.

Being coachable doesn't mean feedback will always feel good. Sometimes criticism stings. But great players separate constructive feedback from personal attacks. They use it as fuel rather than a wound. In life, the ability to take correction without crumbling builds resilience and character.

In football, coaches are the overseers of the team, wearing the headsets and carrying clipboards. In life, "coaches" come in many forms: teachers, mentors, bosses, trusted friends, athletic coaches, or even experiences. The key is recognizing wisdom when it shows up and choosing to learn from it.

Being coachable is about growth over comfort, progress over pride. It's the recognition that learning never stops and that every piece of feedback is an opportunity to level up. The most successful players—and people—are those who never stop being coachable.

Life Drills: Becoming More Coachable

1. Active Listening Drill

In your next conversation, focus entirely on listening without interrupting. Afterward, summarize what you heard before sharing your response.

2. Feedback Journal Drill

Each week, write down one piece of feedback you received (positive or negative) and what you did with it. Track your growth over time.

3. Ask for Coaching Drill

Choose one area of life (school, work, athletics, health, relationships) and ask someone you trust for advice or feedback. Write down their response and commit to applying at least one suggestion.

4. Pause Before Defending Drill

When given feedback, practice pausing for a few seconds instead of defending yourself right away. This helps you absorb the message instead of reacting emotionally.

5. Small Adjustment Drill

Take one piece of feedback and apply a small change immediately—whether in posture, tone of voice, work habit, or daily routine. Train yourself to act quickly on advice.

CHAPTER 13

THE FIELD YOU'RE ON: THE POWER OF YOUR ENVIRONMENT

The Power of Home Field Advantage

In football, we often talk about home field advantage. There's a reason why teams fight for it during playoffs, because where you play matters. The crowd, the noise, the energy, the familiarity of the turf—it all adds up. But beyond stadium lights and scoreboards, the principle behind home field advantage speaks to something much deeper. Just like on the gridiron, the environment you operate in off the field can shape how you perform, grow, and navigate the game of life.

The Power of The Locker Room

Step into any locker room, and you can feel the atmosphere almost immediately. Some are buzzing with camaraderie and accountability, where players push each other to be their best. Others are heavy with tension, blame, and ego. That energy seeps into everything, affecting practices, game day performance, and even team unity.

Life is no different. The people you surround yourself with, in the "locker room" of your life, can either elevate you or drain you. When you're around those who are driven, positive, and supportive, it becomes easier to chase your goals. You start to think bigger, work harder, and believe more. But if your circle is filled with negativity, complacency, or even subtle discouragement, it can slowly chip away at your potential.

The Power of Leaders

Every player knows how critical a coach is. Not just in calling plays, but in creating a culture. A good coach sees more in you than you see in yourself. They hold you accountable, believing in your ability to rise.

In life, mentors, teachers, and leaders play a similar role. The right voices can challenge you in the best ways. But the wrong voices, those who lead with fear, who tear down instead of building up, can make you second-guess your worth. The key is learning to recognize who's coaching your life and whether they deserve that position.

The Power of Response to Circumstances

Ever played on a muddy field? Or in freezing rain? The condition of the weather can change everything. Execution becomes harder. Mistakes are more likely. But the best teams learn to adjust. They stay mentally tough, protect the ball, and adapt their strategy.

The same is true in our lives. Not every circumstance is

ideal. Sometimes you're dealt tough conditions. Maybe it's a toxic workplace, a broken home, or a community lacking support. These situations test your resilience. And just like on the field, you can't always control the conditions, but you *can* control your response. Do you panic or pivot? Do you make excuses or make adjustments?

The Power of The Home Crowd

While on the football field, there's nothing like hearing the road of a home crowd. They lift you when you're tired. They believe in you when the score's against you. They are your support system, which truly matters. In real life, your "home crowd" might be your family, your teammates, or even a friend who reminds you of your purpose.

But what happens when the stands are empty? Or worse, when you feel as if the people in your life are booing instead of cheering you on? During these times you have to ask yourself: Do I have the support I need to get through this season? Are the people around me building me up, or breaking me down?

The Power of The Right System

Sometimes, no matter how talented you are, you're simply in the wrong system. The plays don't suit your strengths. The coaches don't see your value. The culture doesn't match your mindset. In those moments, the bravest thing you can do is switch fields. Change your environment. It doesn't mean you're quitting. It means you're choosing to grow where you can thrive. Life's too short to play in a system that keeps you small.

The Power of Your Environment

In football and in life, your environment influences your mindset, your motivation, and your momentum. The field you're on, the team you're with, the coaches guiding you, they all shape your experience.

So, take stock. Look around. Ask the hard questions. Because if you want to play at your highest level, you need to be in an environment that brings out your best. And if you're not? It's never too late to find a new field.

Life Drills: The Power of Your Environment

1. Locker Room Audit Drill

Make a list of the five people you spend the most time with. Ask yourself: *Do they build me up or pull me down?* Intentionally spend more time with those who challenge and encourage you.

2. Film Study of Surroundings Drill

Walk through your daily spaces — bedroom, workspace, car. Are they cluttered or clear? Energizing or draining? Remove one distraction and add one positive element (like a motivational quote, clean space, or light).

3. Accountability Partner Drill

Choose one person you trust to hold you accountable to a goal. Share your fears about the goal, then what excites you about the goal. Share your progress towards your weekly, just like teammates do in practice.

4. Noise Check Drill

Pay attention to what you consume — music, tv shows, podcasts, social media. Is it sharpening you or dulling you? Replace at least one negative input with something positive and growth focused.

5. Culture Creation Daily Drill

Each morning, set one intention for how you'll shape your environment — it could be encouraging someone, cleaning your space, or setting a tone of positivity at work or home. Over time, these small efforts create a winning culture wherever you go.

CHAPTER 14

DOING THE LITTLE THINGS RIGHT

In football, it's easy to get caught up in the big plays, the touchdowns, the interceptions, and the highlight reels. Those moments are exciting, but any successful player or coach will tell you that games aren't won in just those flashy moments. They're won in the small daily details, the footwork on a block, the angle of pursuit on defense, the timing of a snap count. The little things, repeated with discipline, create the foundation for big victories.

Life works the same way. Most people focus on life's milestones, such as graduating, landing a job, buying a house, or reaching a long awaited goal. But those milestones don't happen without the small, often overlooked daily steps that build to those milestone moments. The "little" moments of waking up early to intentionally prepare for a productive day, or keeping your word when no one's watching, or doing the work even when you don't feel like it is what leads up to success during the "flashy" moments of life.

I remember a coach who drilled us endlessly on something as simple as getting into our stance the right way. At the time, it felt tedious. I asked myself, "Why spend so much time on something so basic?" But later, in a critical game, I realized how those details mattered. A proper stance gave me the balance to hold my ground and the leverage to win the battle in front of me. One small detail set the stage for a big moment.

In life, the "stance" might look different. It could consist of double-checking your work before you turn it in. Maybe it's listening fully when someone is speaking. Perhaps it's taking care of your health before it breaks down. These actions don't grab headlines, but they make the difference between barely getting by and truly excelling.

Doing the little things right also builds trust. In football, when a teammate knows you'll take care of your assignment, they can focus on theirs. In life, when people see you consistently handling the details, they trust you with bigger responsibilities. That level of trust opens doors that talent alone cannot.

The truth is, anyone can show up for the big moments. But the people who truly succeed, in football and in life, are the ones who commit to the little things every single day. They understand that greatness isn't built on luck or shortcuts. It's built on small habits done well, over and over again.

So, whether you're lacing up your cleats or walking into a new opportunity, remember...the little things aren't little.

They're everything!

Life Drills: Doing the Little Things Right

1. The Stance Check Drill

Just like lining up correctly before a play, take one extra minute before any task — a meeting, an assignment, even a conversation — to review your "stance." Ask: *Am I ready? Do I have what I need at this moment?* This habit sets the foundation for success before the action begins.

2. The Follow-Through Drill

Pick one small commitment (returning calls, finishing workouts, making your bed) and do it without fail for 30 days. Like finishing a play until the whistle blows, this trains you to value completion, not just effort.

3. Film Detail Study Drill

In football, film reveals missed details. In life, reflection does the same. At the end of the day, write down one detail you handled well and one you missed. Over time, patterns will emerge that help you sharpen your habits.

4. The Assignment Drill

Choose one responsibility in work, school, or family and commit to owning it fully with no excuses and no shortcuts. Just like a player who handles their assignment every down, you'll earn trust by showing dependability.

5. Small Wins Drill

Each morning, complete two small intentional actions (like stretching, journaling, or sending a thoughtful message). Small wins early create momentum for the bigger challenges ahead in the day.

CHAPTER 15

CALM IN THE CHAOS: CONTROLLING YOUR EMOTIONS IN FOOTBALL AND LIFE

Football is a game of physical collisions, mental collisions, and emotional collisions. Every snap brings intensity. A bad call from the referee, a hard hit from an opponent, or even a teammate's mistake can spark frustration. But the great players, the ones you trust in critical moments, are not those who let emotions take over. The great players are the ones who stay calm, think clearly, and respond with discipline.

In football, emotional control is often the difference between victory and defeat. A late hit born out of anger can cost your team fifteen yards. Losing focus due to frustration can cause a missed assignment. Football teaches us that when emotions control you, they often work against you. But when you control them, you unlock composure, resilience, and clarity.

Think about quarterback Tom Brady in the fourth quarter of tight games. No matter the score or the noise, he never looked rushed. His teammates often said his calmness gave them confidence. He treated every drive the same way, focusing on execution and not emotion. That poise under pressure helped turn deficits into legendary comebacks. Brady's greatness wasn't just in his arm; it was in his ability to control himself when everything around him was chaotic.

On the defensive side, emotional control is just as important. Imagine a cornerback getting pushed after the whistle. The easy thing to do would be to shove back, but the smart thing is to walk away. A retaliation flag can extend the drive, cost field position, and shift momentum. The best defenders know that their job isn't to fight emotionally, it's to fight strategically. They let their play speak, not their tempers.

Life isn't much different. The world throws challenges at you every single day through differences of perspectives at work, negative encounters at school, traffic that tests your patience, and out of the blue setbacks. Like in football, when life tests you, it's not the circumstances themselves that define you, but how you respond to them. Do you react impulsively, or do you breathe, reset, and move forward with purpose?

Great quarterbacks don't just throw touchdowns, they manage pressure. Great defenders don't just make tackles, they manage their emotions. Great leaders in life do the same. Emotional control and the ability to manage life's pressures are forms of leadership. Emotional intelligence and self-control builds trust. It steadies the people around you. It helps you see solutions when others only see problems.

Football teaches us that emotions are natural, but they don't have to control us. Discipline, patience, and composure aren't signs of weakness; they're the ultimate strength. When you can keep your cool in the heat of competition or the chaos of life, you give yourself and those around you the best chance to win.

Life Drills: Training Emotional Control

1. The Reset & Breath Drill

Just as players reset between plays, take one deep breath before responding to a stressful situation. Give yourself space before reacting.

2. The 24-Hour Rule Drill

Don't make big decisions or send intense messages in the heat of emotion. Wait, cool down, then act with clarity.

3. Focus on the Next Play Drill

In football, you can't dwell on a fumble. In life, you can't dwell on mistakes. Shift your energy to what comes next.

4. Lead by Composure Drill

Whether in the huddle, in your home, at school, or out and about remember that you have the ability to set the tone.

Others will follow your calm.

5. Identifying Triggers Drill

Whenever you feel yourself becoming frustrated, upset or angry, practice mindfulness to locate how you feel in the moment and what may be causing you to feel the way you do. Then focus on calming down and reframing your thoughts. Take a moment to choose how to respond to your trigger. This helps you move from unconscious reactions to intentional responses, building greater emotional intelligence and improving your ability to handle challenging situations.

CONCLUSION

GAME TIME!

Now that you have gained such vital information and awareness, the ball is now in your hands to put this knowledge into practice and make a play. Do the work and get legitimate results in your life.

This book is not the be-all and end-all. It does, however, provide you with valuable tools to keep you on your journey to success. The next step is for you to practice putting the Life Drills to use, then build upon them. The ultimate goal is for you to sharpen your skills and execute with precision in life. Remain disciplined by perfecting your daily routine, and when things get tough tap into your will to win.

You've been given essential skills to win in life. Remember the importance of effective communication, keep in mind how to handle adversity, create and know intently your life's playbook, assess your huddle and your environment, pay attention to the small details, remain disciplined, and control your emotions.

Choose to move in life with clarity and confidence knowing you have done, and are continuing to do, the work. And don't be afraid to share your newfound skills with others. Teaching and displaying your skills to someone else also holds you accountable to executing those skills. So, if you know anyone who could benefit from the knowledge you've obtained, don't gatekeep. Honor the principle of giving, and you shall continue to receive what you need.

Show up ready for opportunities that you desire in this life. Crush your goals, and simply be the great, well-rounded, balanced, and fulfilled human being you were created to be.

Tap in! You got this...I believe in you!

ACKNOWLEDGEMENTS

I would like to first and foremost acknowledge God for gifting me with athleticism, the love for the game of football, the skill to exegete the game, and the ability to make a difference in the lives of the next generation. It's not by might, nor by power, but by the Spirt of God that I do this work (Zechariah 4:6).

To my wife, Santisha, thank you for being so understanding as I give of myself to this game that I've been blessed to play, coach, and teach the next generation. The days are extensive, and the work is never ending. I'm grateful that I get to freely operate in this gift with your unwavering support.

To my parents, I appreciate you supporting me and my love for this game at every level, from might mites to college. I'm appreciative of the foundation you have provided and the backing you have shown. I'm also thankful for my dad passing the passion for the game of football down in my DNA.

To Uncle Al, you have shared the love for the game of football with me since I can remember. I'm grateful for your

continued support as I expand my reach as a football coach. You have watched me grow as both a football player and a coach, and I'm appreciative that I now get to continue to be a part of this game with you and your sons by my side.

To my football and flag football teammates over the years. We've had amazing times together and memories we will treasure forever. I'm grateful to have played such a challenging, yet rewarding, game alongside each of you.

To every coach I've had the pleasure of playing under, from mighty mites to college. You each instilled a lesson in me that I cherish even today. Thank you for your dedication to the game of football.

To every football, and flag football, player I've had the privilege of coaching. We've shared proud moments as well as tough moments, and we have each learned valuable lessons. I'm proud of the progress I have witnessed, and I pray nothing but the best for each of you.

To the coaches I've had the pleasure of standing on the sidelines with over the years. The days are long and the work never ends, but we continue to do the work, and we remain committed. Specifically, I would like to acknowledge the Carolina United Flag Football Club coaches who are dedicated to CU's mission and whose love for the game and players never wavers. I'm appreciative to be on this journey with each of you.

To the Co-founders of Carolina United Flag Football Club,

Alain Valaka, Dominique Boyd, and Jeremy Ashe. We were teammates over 17 years ago, and we took a leap of faith to start CU over 8 years ago. It's been an honor serving alongside each of you as we work to fulfill the mission. The bond formed has been nothing short of amazing. I'm grateful to call each of you my brother.

ABOUT THE AUTHOR

errick A. Walker, also known as Coach Walk, has been a dynamic football coach for over 17 years. He is not only a lover of the game, but considered a football connoisseur as well. Having played since childhood, Derrick is enthusiastic about all things football, but also comprehends the game on an expertise level. His deep knowledge and passion have allowed him to serve as a go-to for not only traditional football teams, but also as a point of reference for the up-and-coming flag football world.

Derrick expresses, "Ever since I was 8 years old, I've had a natural attraction to football. The love of the game was passed down to me from my dad, grandma, and uncle. From starting at the mighty mite level to playing in college, to coaching high-school students and adults, football has always been a part of my life. I'm grateful that I now get to give back and help the next generation get better at the game, while simultaneously learning life skills to succeed in life. I also get to play a pivotal part in promoting flag football across the country, which means a lot to me."

Derrick has served as Co-founder and Executive Director of Carolina United Flag Football Club (CU) since 2017, with a mission for CU to be the premier club team for athletes desiring to experience competitive flag football while giving back to their local communities. He also gives back as an Elite Wide Receiver and Defensive Back skills trainer. Derrick serves as a community leader and youth mentor to local high school students through both traditional and flag football. Derrick believes in staying abreast as a football coach, and has obtained his USA Football Coach Certification.

Derrick resides in Raleigh-Durham, North Carolina. When not immersed in football, Derrick is spending time with his wife, traveling, catching up with close friends, golfing, spending time with extended family, and simply enjoying life.

To learn more about Derrick's Elite Wide Receiver and Defensive Back skills training, visit CoachWalk81.com

To connect with Derrick on social media, follow him on Instagram @coach_walk81

To learn more and to support Carolina United Flag Football Club, visit CUFlag.org.